THE AMAZING ELLA

The Inspirational Story of the
First Female Optometrist in the
United States

words and pictures by
Angie P. Baker, O.D.

ACKNOWLEDGEMENT

The story of Dr. Ella Gertrude Stanton was painstakingly researched and compiled into an article by Dr. Viktoria Davis and Dr. Lilien Vogl. Dr. Davis and Dr. Vogl followed Dr. Stanton into the amazing field of Optometry. So did I. I am in their debt for sharing her story with the world and allowing me to share it with kids.

BIBLIOGRAPHY

Davis, V., & Vogl, L. (2019). Gertrude Stanton (1863-1931): The First Woman Licensed to Practice Optometry in the United States. Hindsight: Journal of Optometry History, 51(1), 5–10.

DEDICATION

In deepest gratitude to God for leading me to the work that I love. To my dad who told me I could be anything I wanted to be. And, to my girls, take small steps towards big dreams.

Library of Congress Control Number: 2024922055

ISBN
Hardcover 979-8-9914205-2-5
Paperback 979-8-9914205-3-2

This is Dr. Ella Gertrude Stanton.
The girl who made glasses.

Ella became the first female eye
doctor in the United States.

She was a pioneer who
insisted on equality.

This is Ella. Ella grew up in Iowa with at least six brothers and sisters... and maybe a dog.

Girls Ella's age were expected to learn to sew and cook.

But, Ella learned to make glasses.

She had great attention to detail and a talent for fixing things.

Ella lived at a time when not many moms went to college. That didn't stop Ella.

At the age of 30 and as a mother of three she earned her first college degree.

She was confident and intelligent.

I'm impressed.

With Ella...not with the hat.

Me too.

If you'd just turn the page... please.

I'll just need a little help.

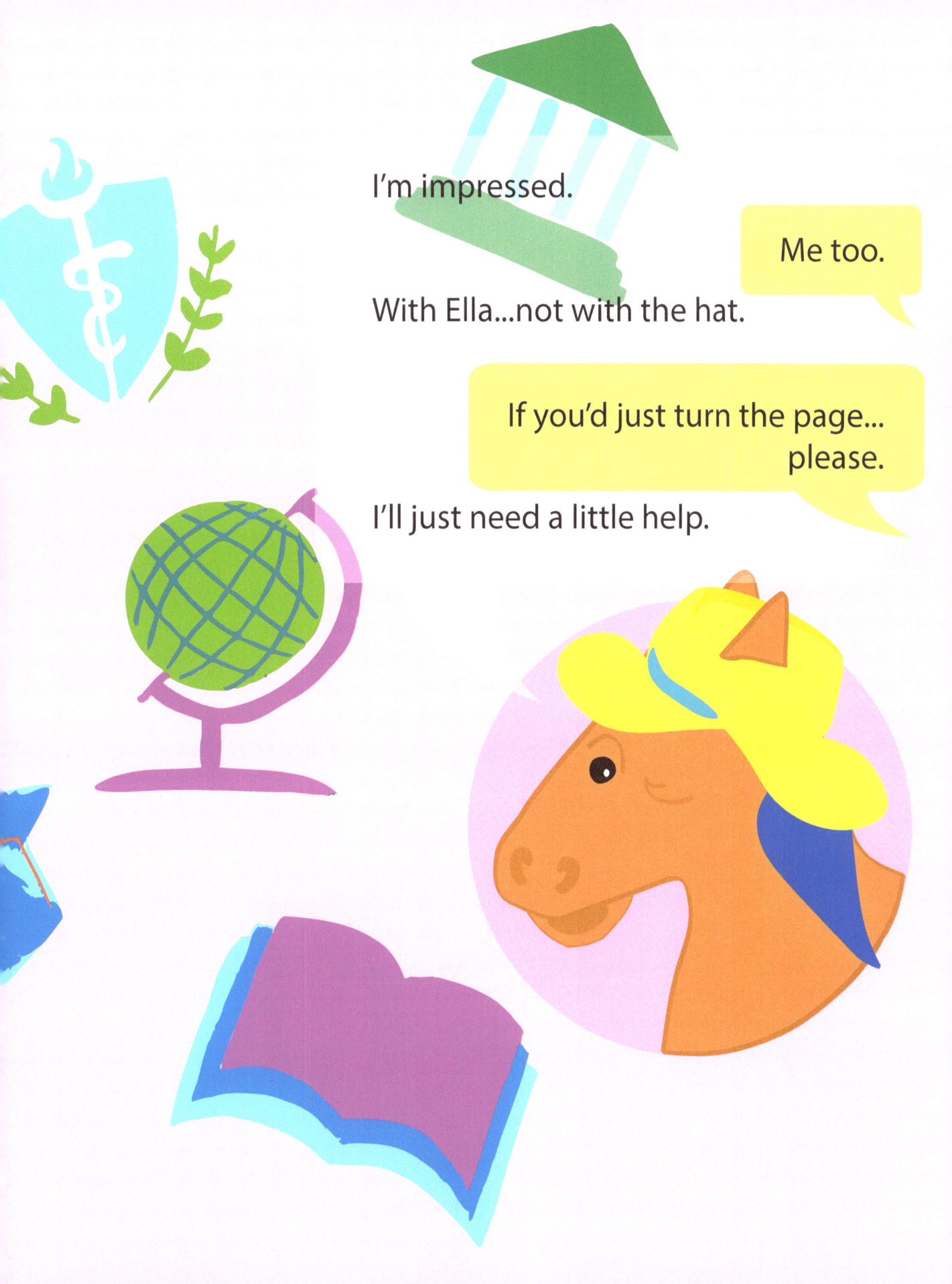

Later, Ella left home and traveled around Minnesota, making and selling glasses.

Before rolling into town, she would advertise her expertise and amazing glasses.

She was courageous and bold.

So, the hat was her idea.

Yes. It would catch people's attention. You know... marketing.

Well, now we have social media. So, can we lose the hat?

Just for you.

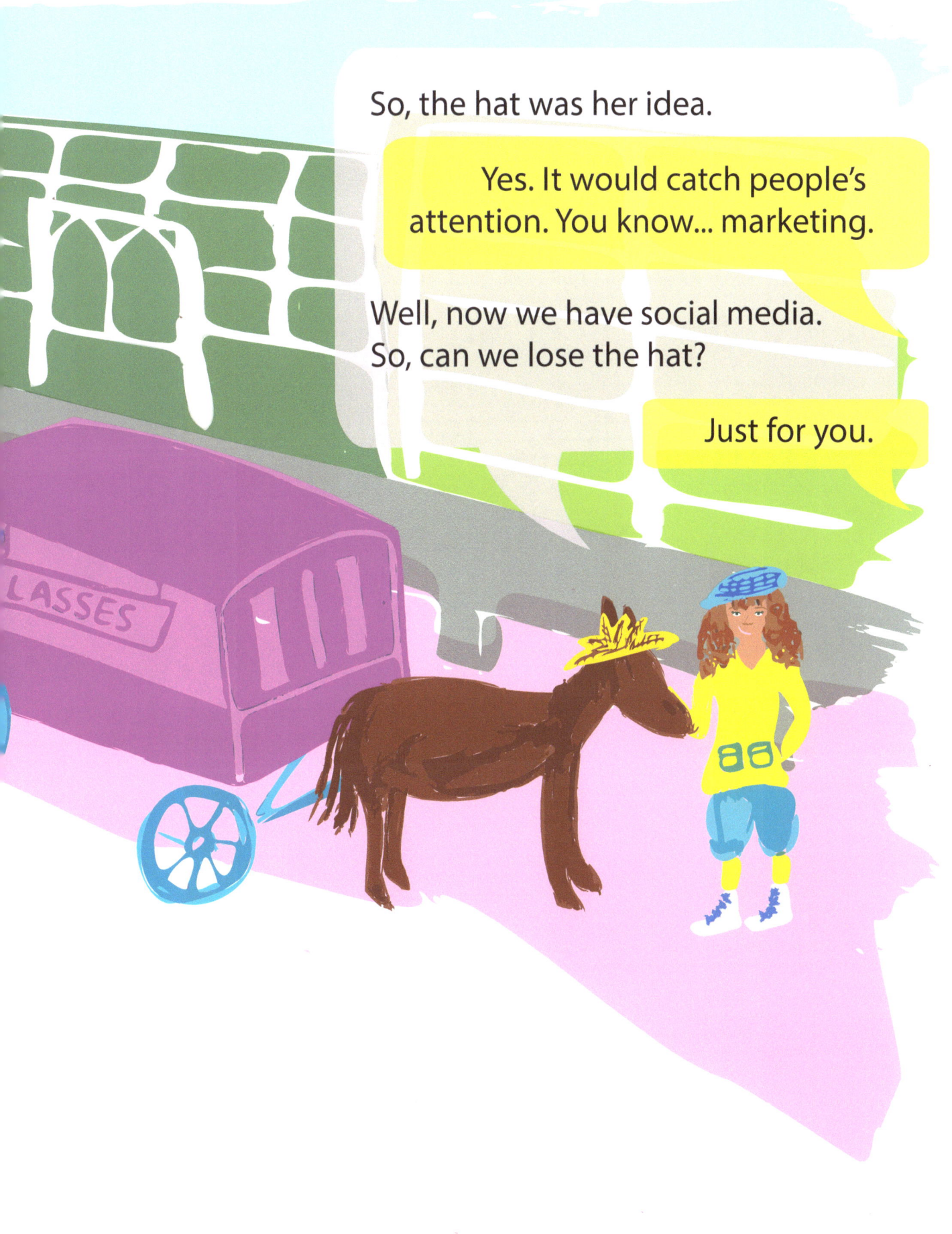

Ella was really good at making glasses and making sure people had healthy eyes.

Soon, it became a law that you had to get a license to do those things.

Many men applied but only a few women. Ella applied and became the FIRST woman eye doctor in the US!

She was proud and a pioneer

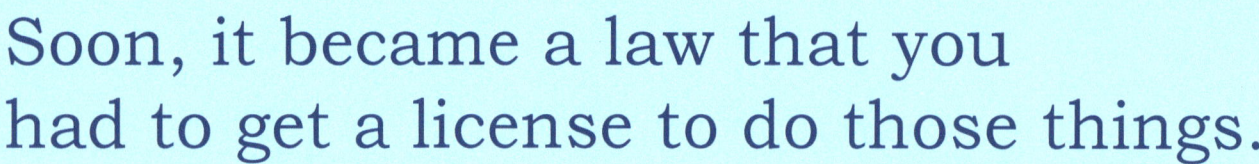

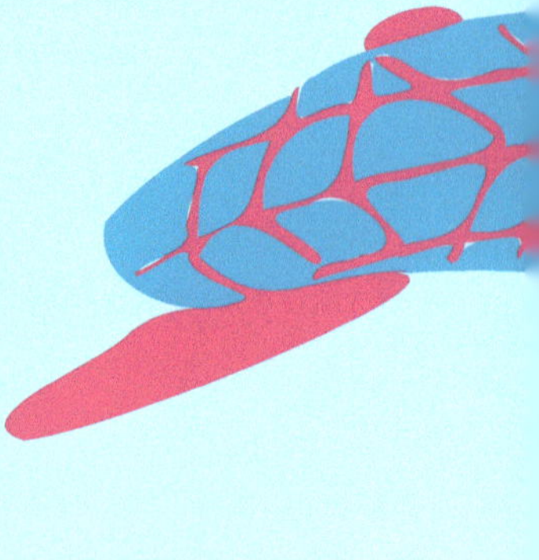

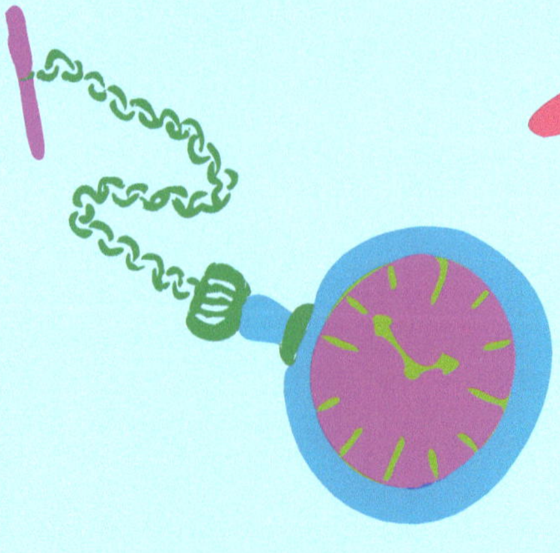

Eventually, Ella opened her own business in Minneapolis, checking eyes and making glasses.

At that time in history, women could get paid less for what they made and what they knew.

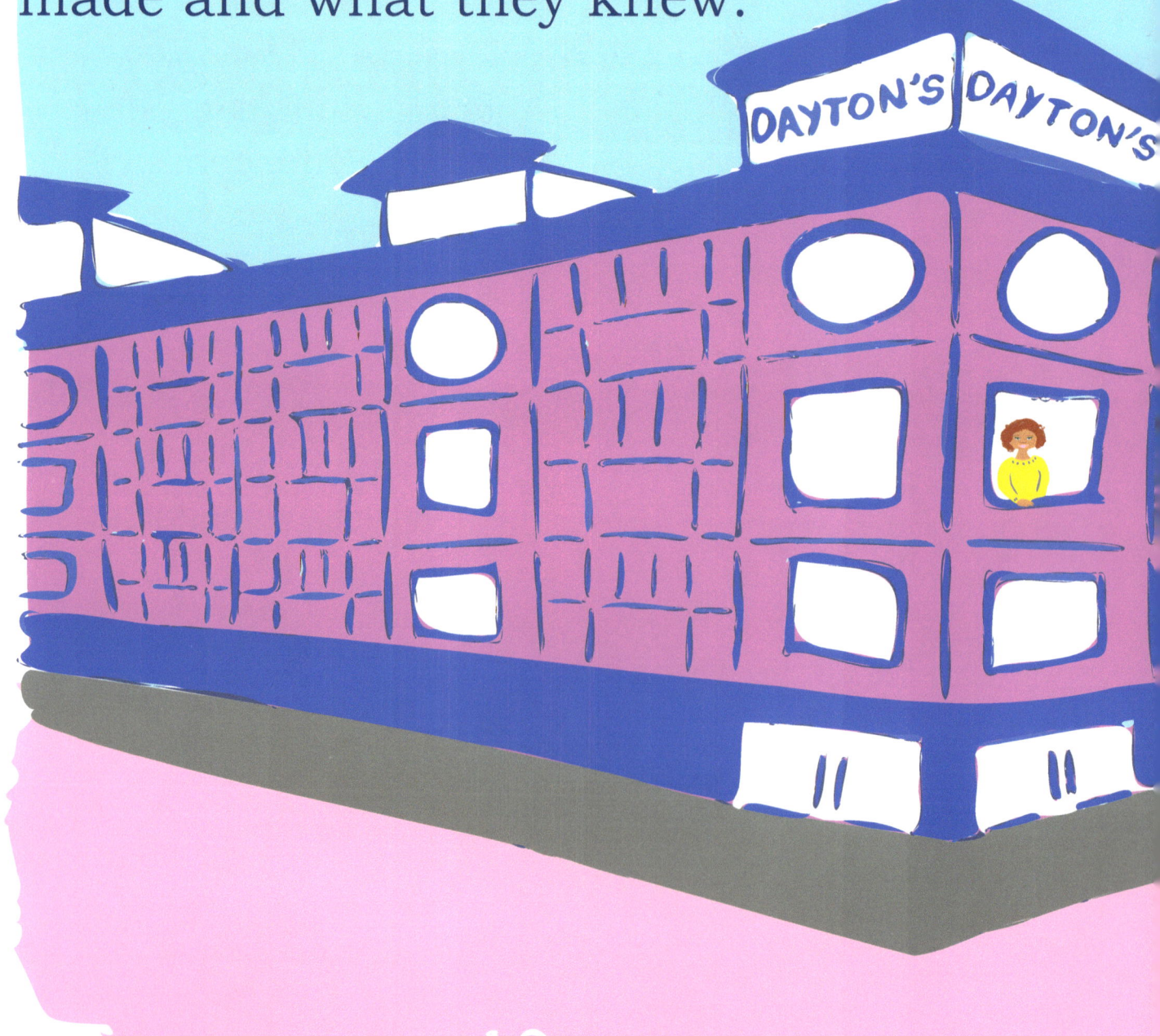

Ella insisted she get paid fairly for her knowledge of eyes and the glasses she made.

Ella was tenacious and successful.

Ella didn't just work for herself.
She also helped in her community.

She was so popular that she once raised
the most money in a contest for the local
newspaper. The prize was a new car!

Ella was spunky and outgoing.

Wait a minute! Did that car just take my job?

Cars were a historic innovation. Ella was always moving with the times.

What possible advantage does a car have over a majestic animal like myself?

Cars don't...

Don't say it. You have a point.

Ella continued learning everything she could about eyes and helped the new profession of Optometry grow.

She wrote and published articles to educate others.

She was innovative and an advocate.

Ella looked to the future closer to home as well. Her daughter, Sadie, became an optometrist and they worked together for many years.

Ella was inspiring and influential.

This is Dr. Ella Gertrude Stanton-the girl who made glasses, the pioneer who became the first female eye doctor in the United States, and, the leader who lives on in history to inspire you and generations to come.

Wow! I look great in glasses.

DR. GERTRUDE STANTON, Minnesota.

1863 February 17 or 26, Ella Gertrude Smith born in Howard County, Iowa

1880 October 30, Ella marries Roswell Eugene Ayer

1881 Ella's son Arthur Darius is born

1884 Ella's daughter Sarah (Sadie) Taylor is born

1890 Ella receives Dakota Territory teaching certificate

1891 Ella's son John Herbert is born

1893 Ella earns her first college degree

1899 Ella is working out of Willmar, Minnesota, traveling and making glasses

1901 America's first Optometry Practice Law passes in Minnesota

1901 June, Dr. Ella Gertrude Ayer becomes the first female licensed optometrist in America

1901 December 4, Ella marries Dr. Charles Stanton

1903 March 18, Ella opens her optical service office in Dayton's Dry Goods building

1905 Ella serves as first vice president of the Northwestern Optical Association

1905 Ella is the first female to earn a Doctor of Optics degree from Illinois College of Ophthalmology and Otology

1907 Ella wins a 1907 Oldsmobile in a newspaper popularity contest

1908 Ella presents and publishes the scholarly article "Indications in Retinal Fatigue"

1909 December 8, Ella marries Joseph Jones

1915 Sadie becomes a licensed optometrist and joins Ella in practice

1919 Ella and Sadie receive thanks for acting as consulting optometrist for the US Army Medical Corps during WWI

1920 Ella and Sadie operate an all-female practice and optical shop

1931 March 25, Ella dies of natural causes in California while visiting her son

2020 January, Drs V. Davis and L. Vogl publish Ella's story in HINDSIGHT: *Journal of Optometry History*

When Ella was alive, eyeglasses were made from glass. Now, glasses are made from safer and lighter materials like different kinds of plastic. If you wear glasses to see your best, you can even get your prescription put in sports goggles and scuba masks.

Ella set glasses lenses into metal frames. Now, you can get frames in metal, plastic, or wood. They can be any shape and size. There are even frames that glow in the dark!

The power in lenses is called a prescription. Eyeglasses are designed for just one person, just like medicine from your family doctor. Even though they look amazing, don't try on your friend's glasses.

Ella was an optician that learned to be an eye doctor. Now, there are three distinct specialties involved in taking care of your eyes. **OPTICIANS** specialize in making glasses. **OPTOMETRISTS** are eye doctors that work with you to prescribe glasses and take care of the health of your eyes. **OPHTHALMOLOGISTS** are eye doctors that specialize in surgery.

To become an Optometrist like Ella in the United States, you need to study science and math in high school and college. After graduating college, you need to complete Optometry school and pass tests to prove you are qualified to take care of others' eyes. In 2024 there are 24 Optometric colleges in the United States and Puerto Rico.

"It is a woman's failing to underestimate the value in dollars and cents of what she does...It is essential, of course, that not only the actual cost of an article but that one's experience, one's expenses and one's brains should enter into the fixing of prices for whatever one puts on the market."

-Dr. Ella Gertrude Stanton, 1863-1931

Those are cool bubble wands.

Those are trial lenses and early types of glasses, like Ella made. Glasses look much different now, but trial lenses that helped Ella determine a patient's glasses prescription are still used today by eye doctors like me.

Wait! You're an eye doctor? I suddenly like you better.

And, I love your glasses.

www.ingramcontent.com/pod-product-compliance
Lightning Source LLC
Chambersburg PA
CBHW041620120626
46551CB00003B/517